# CRINKLED 'N' WR~~INKLED~~

BUT STILL YOUNG AT HEART!

by Anthony

First Published in Great Britain by
Powerfresh Limited
3 Gray Street
Northampton
England
NN1 3QQ

Telephone 01604 30996 Country Code 44
Facsimile 01604 21013

CRINKLED 'N' WRINKLED
ISBN 1 874125 17 1

Printed in Britain by Avalon Print Ltd., Northampton.

# AVOID EVEN **BIGGER** SHOCKS....

# A GOOD WAY OF STAYING YOUNG IS TO MIX WITH PEOPLE YOUNGER THAN YOURSELF...

# NEVER READ OBITUARY COLUMNS...

# IT'S A FACT....

YOU KNOW YOU'RE GETTING OLD WHEN WOMEN REFER TO YOU AS '**CUDDLY**'

TRY AND GET EIGHT HOURS
SLEEP A NIGHT....

(PREFERABLY IN BED!)

# IT'S A FACT....

THE OLDER YOU
GET, THE BETTER
YOU LOOK WITH
CLOTHES ON!

SOME WOMEN PREFER THE
MORE MATURE MAN....

# TAKE UP A HOBBY...

BEING OLD DOESN'T MAKE YOU ANY
BETTER AT PICKING WINNERS....

# SPEND MORE TIME IN THE GARDEN....

First Published in Great Britain by
Powerfresh Limited
3 Gray Street
Northampton
England
NN1 3QQ

Telephone 01604 30996 Country Code 44
Facsimile 01604 21013

CRINKLED 'N' WRINKLED
ISBN 1 874125 17 1

Printed in Britain by Avalon Print Ltd., Northampton.